Walking the East End:
A Historic African-American Community in West Chester, Pennsylvania

A self-guided walking tour of West Chester's historic African-American community.

By Sarah Wesley and Catherine C. Quillman

Acknowledgements

By Catherine C. Quillman

Numerous people were involved in this project, which began as a small walking tour written by Sarah in the mid-1990s. This includes the staff at the Charles A. Melton Arts and Education Center, who lent us old slides and rare activity programs so that we could copy them for use in our book. We also want to thank David Jones of the Capt. Levi M. Hood Lodge, Lenny Closson of the Star Social Club, and members of the Star of West Tent.

Unless otherwise noted, all the contemporary photography in the book is by Janice I. Houck, who worked more than a year on the project. A big thank you.

The bulk of our research was found at the Chester County Historical Society. We are most grateful to Pam Powell, the historical society's photo archivist who waved the photography fees. Due to space restraints, we were unable to identify the donor of every photo. However, the following people helped us obtain photos: Sherry Wade, Ernest Irons, Sylvia Kenion, Alice Hammond, Mary Ann Champion, Marietta Barnes, Helen Betty Ringgold, Wesley Adderton, Jr. and George London.

Many of the 1960s photos of buildings and streets were taken by the late John Clark. A special thanks to the artist Dane Tilghman, who photographed many family albums. Cris Staley Hutchinson, whose husband's shop, Rose Valley Restorations, is located in the "Mechanics Alley," also supplied her photography talents. All the early postcards in the book were loaned to us by William Supplee. The beautiful photo montages were by Amanda Craig and Peggy Hartzell, who directs the photography department at the Henderson High School.

Several residents supplied us with specific information: Harry Parrish, who gave us the history of Rice's Temple Church, Renee Cookie Washington, the historian for St. Paul's Baptist Church, and Leon Spriggs who loaned us photos and told us the lively history of the "Royal Palace."

We are grateful to Jim Jones, who not only supplied us with a list of all the Bayard Rustin homes, he maintains a web site and has written extensively about the area. One book cited in the introduction is *West Chester to 1865: That Elegant & Notorious Place* by Douglas R. Harper.

Book production by Tracy Colletto Adams, Cover and book design by Caroline Chen at www.chengraphix.com
Copyright ©2012 Catherine C. Quillman and Sarah Wesley, Second Edition
All rights reserved.
Library of Congress Control Number:ISBN-13: 978-0615629452 (Hedgerow Press)
ISBN-10: 0615629458

Author's Note

About the "East End" Name

The historian Jim Jones, who wrote a book about West Chester's early railroads, has observed that the borough didn't see any growth until the age of steam, in the early 1800s. Naturally, the early industries here – the coal, lumber and "spoke works" – were located along railroad corridors. As Jones describes it, they became early boundaries, defining the "other side of the tracks," such as the East End. Other historians have traced the early black community to John George, an abolitionist and temperance crusader who rented homes clustered around the corner of South Franklin and East Market to black residents beginning in 1848. Newspaper reporters as early as 1859 described the area "George's corner," or "Georgetown," until eventually, in the mid-1870s, the entire East Ward east of the railroad was known as "Georgetown." By the late 19th century, the area was the largest black neighborhood in West Chester.

About the maps:

The individual maps on each page of this book are from a map published in 1883. The map published separately features two additional tours (the "Uptown" and the "Industrial" tours), and is the work of cartographer, Pamela Goffinet. She can be reached through her web site at www.pamgoffinet.com

Photo credits marked "CCHS" represent the Chester County Historical Society, West Chester, PA.

Under the leadership of Bayard Rustin, protesters of a fair housing demonstration in 1966 met the community center and marched along East Miner street (pictured near the South Franklin intersection) on their way to the court house downtown. Photo courtesy of CCHS

The collages on the next page and pg.99 are by Peggy Harzell

Introduction

In the years following the Civil War, black-owned businesses were an accepted part of the West Chester business community, and they often claimed the best locations – in the center of town.

In 1870, business was booming for restaurateur James Spence. Spence's Restaurant was housed in an elaborate structure he built on East Gay Street, where a trolley line rattled by its Palladian windows and a large staff served up steaming portions of house specialties such as oyster stew, fried clams, and snapper soup. You could say Spence's success was just another sign of the entrepreneurial times except for one fact: he was a black man.

James Spence

In the years following the Civil War, black-owned businesses were an accepted part of the West Chester business community, and they often claimed the best locations – in the center of town. In addition to Spence's Restaurant, there was Burns' Great Oyster House on West Gay Street and Fortune Fullerton's oyster bar in the exclusive Mansion Hotel on Market Street. And a man named George Ganges went about town, selling ice cream from a horse-drawn cart.

As the county seat, West Chester in the 1800s drew people from the surrounding farming community. It was also a commercial hub comprising some of the region's largest enterprises, many of them in the East End, such as Uriah Painter's ice pond, Hoopes Bros. and Darlington Wheel Factory, and Edward Jacobs Inc., an early mushroom cannery. Yet judging from the 1883 Breous "farm" atlas, West Chester was a place that mixed industrial sites such as rail depots and lumber yards with hotels and florist shops.

The concept of a "downtown" or a neighborhood on the "other side of the tracks" had yet to become part of the public lexicon. As early as 1833, for instance, a rail terminus was located at the corner of East Chestnut and North Matlack Streets. Another depot, built in 1836 on East Gay Street, was two doors down from Spence's Restaurant.

Although Spence's proximity to depot or the Court House does not appear in any of

An early West Chester couple

the surviving advertisements, the old real estate adage about the importance of location seems to be relevant. Spence's was not only was popular, it catered to the borough's professional elite – its judges and lawyers – as well as to a group typically excluded from restaurants at the time: women. Although it was considered improper for a woman to eat away from home, in a public place, Spence offered a solution. A series of advertisements in the 1870s announced that "a private saloon for the ladies" was available on the restaurant's second floor, while ice cream was made on the premises and meals were served "at all hours of the day."

Presumably, the black business owners felt emboldened by the town's Quaker heritage and its reputation for racial tolerance. The historian Doug Harper has observed that the borough, a major settlement above the Mason & Dixon Line, had a "keen" awareness of the slavery "debates" before and during the Civil War. Living so close to slave territory in Maryland and Delaware, black residents were understandably cautious about making waves and typically expressed gratitude – for their good fortune in business or in life – in the rare instances they were interviewed by the local reporters. Indeed, there seemed to have been a general agreement in West Chester that lasted through the 19th century that the borough was an accepting place for the free black man. Late in Spence's career as a restaurateur, for instance, a local white resident named Daniel Webster Nields wrote to him: "I am glad to have been born and raised in a community where prejudice found no foothold, where a man's worth in the community was not established by the color of his clothes or the shade of his skin, but by his deportment."

Despite Nields' confidence that West Chester was a place of opportunity for the all men, newspaper accounts suggest that that the black community faced extreme challenges and inequities. Historian Jim Jones puts it this way: "the first three people executed in West Chester were all of African descent…It took eleven more years before a white man (Jabez Boyd) was found guilty of a capital offense, and in all, six of the first nine people executed were black."

Even the esteemed historians "Judge" Futhey and Gilbert Cope were not above some sort of negative commentary. In their 1881 book, *The History of Chester County*, they devote nearly a full page to the life of James Jackson, a former slave. Jones writes: "After noting that the industrious Jackson found construction work with many prominent citizens…the authors noted without irony that Jackson 'retired' in 1877, when he would have been nearly one hundred years old."

James Jackson

Benjamin "Billy" Freeman

The founders of the Star Social Club, circa 1896, in front of Burns' restaurant.

Another former slave, Benjamin Freeman, appears in an account by William P. Townsend. He wrote that around 1831 Freeman rode a team of "five or six fine horses," hauling lumber for Thomas Powell and later plaster mortar for Wm. Louis Shields (of the East End). "Being industrious and economical," in time Freeman was able to obtain his own wagon, pulled by a bull named "Barney," and eventually went into business for himself. He built a two-story brick house, with a shop out back, at 127 West Barnard, "all of which he paid for by his labor aided by the economic habits and industry of his wife."

For the most part, though, the early newspapers did not highlight the kind of entrepreneurship Booker T. Washington promoted – one based on acquisition and accumulation. More common were news items of "colored" vagrants or occasional workers such as the black man handing out flyers in 1880. "He attracted an unusual attention in consequence of his attire, which was of many colors," the item read.

There is unfortunately scant material on Vincent Anderson, an African-American landowner who was so prominent in the 1840s and 1850s, the East End was sometimes called "Andersonville" instead of "Georgetown," after John George, a white landlord. Anderson's son, Osborne Perry Anderson (1830-1872), could be described as one of West Chester's most famous black Abolitionists. Born in West Chester in 1830, Anderson became famous for surviving the raid on Harpers Ferry, Virginia on October 16, 1860. Interestingly the event eclipsed the recent news of the opening of the borough's all-black school, the Adams Street School, when newspapers were reacting positively about the new "negro quarter."

Anderson later wrote an account of his experience with John Brown, A Voice from Harpers Ferry, and renewed his ties to two West Chester residents, Abraham D. Shadd, and his daughter, Mary Ann Shadd (1823-1893), all of whom eventually moved to Canada.

Just prior to the Civil War, the Shadds mentored Anderson and were opposed to the colonization movement that was sending blacks to Liberia.

This early postcard depicts the Zion AME Church at the left of West Miner Street in "Everhart's Grove."

West Chester's main proponent was a black man named Abram Dobson, whose real estate holdings rivaled that of Moses Hepburn, who became West Chester's first black council man in 1882. Curiously, it is not known if Dobson had any influence, but historian Doug Harper has noted that the number of black residents dropped "relative to the rest of the borough – from 14 percent in 1850 to less than 12 percent in 1860."

The mixed reception the black community often received is perhaps reflected in its early organizations, schools, and churches, which typically moved from place to place, renting various rooms in West Chester. One of the oldest black organizations in the state, the Star Social Club, was founded in 1896 and did not have a permanent location (its present-day location on East Market Street) until 1953.

The oldest black church in the borough, the Bethel AME Church, did not have a building of its own for a generation after its founding. A short item about the church's founding in the 1835 Centennial Souvenir hints of the difficulties faced by the congregation, who laid a cornerstone on West Market Street – on a lot later deemed unsuitable. The item says nothing more than the ceremony took place "in the pouring rain…with many people [soaked] to the skin,"

Historian Doug Harper has written that Bethel (then known as Zion AME) was persuaded to relocate to West Miner Street, in an area called "Everhart's Grove," but that proved too far away from the growing black community in the East End. Hinting at an apparent rift in the congregation in 1861, a news account announced that "Zion" had split and a new church, known as

"Little Pat Foot" later St. Luke's – was actively looking for a new location. Both churches eventually relocated to the East End.

Around 1851, early black residents pushed for the construction of the first black school – Harmony School – but it was built on West Barnard Street, blocks away from the East End. Eventually, in 1856, the school board of West Chester agreed that a new school was needed, and the Adams Street School was built at the corner of South Adams and East Barnard Streets. The concept of building such a school, at public expense, so that the "colored children of this borough were provided for," as the newspapers put it, was a radical concept. However, the school struggled for years with "leftovers" from the white schools, and controversy later erupted over student segregation. In the words of Charles H. Burns, who formed a committee of protest in 1894, "it is not right to compel us to send children from the neighborhood of one school to another," he asserted, "and we intend to have this practice stopped if we can."

In his history of West Chester, Doug Harper gives an account of the East End in a chapter titled "Life in Georgetown." Harper describes the East End as typical of all of West Chester, observing that much of the town in the 1850s was "Southern" in character, with new town houses being built with wide piazzas down one side and balconies adorned with wrought-iron. The black community itself contributed to this Southern flavor since nearly one-third of black residents in 1850 census were born in slave states ("though not necessarily in slavery," Harper adds).

Gay Street School

The gradual segregation of West Chester could easily be viewed as a result of the growth of new neighborhoods in the 1840s – ones that black residents could not afford – but Harper adds that black residents had a good reason for moving to the East End. "It was conscious and deliberate: African Americans were withdrawing from increasingly hostile social institutions and community."

Children, circa 1965

Those "hostile" elements included the Chester County courts and a complex licensing system that required applicants to re-apply each year, with a description of why the business was needed and a "tavern" petition filled with signatures of support from local residents. When Moses Hepburn filed

5

his application to open his East End hotel on February 4, 1868, he pleaded that "said borough stands in pressing need of an inn or tavern for the entertainment of people of color." In an even bolder move, Hepburn added "that the public houses now established refuse to entertain this class of people visiting this town, and are consequently driven to seek accommodations in [sic] private families or inconvenient places."

Of all the black entrepreneurs, Hepburn was probably the least dependent on the white community. His father, also named Moses, was a slave who had been "liberated by his [white] paternal parent," as one paper described it, and later raised a family and accumulated a small fortune in real estate holdings in Alexandria, Virginia. Around 1818, Hepburn Senior came to West Chester for a short period of time, in part to receive the education denied to former slaves in Virginia.

After his white father left him a "bequest of several thousand dollars," Hepburn, Sr. sent his own son, Moses Garrison, to Washington, D.C., where he received an education under the auspices of the AME Church. Apparently, this was considered an act of defiance, for the Virginia authorities were said to have threatened Hepburn's ability to conduct business, and the family returned to the more hospitable atmosphere of West Chester in 1847. Not much is known about Hepburn Senior in the borough, although he did describe his occupation as a "gentleman" in the 1860 census, the year before his death. His estate sustained his family for generations: It had $9,000 in real estate holdings and $30,000 in personal property. The younger Hepburn received one-third of the estate, as did his four siblings.

Hepburn took his share and built the "Magnolia House" – a Southern-style hotel with a piazza overlooking South Franklin Street – and ran it for 30 years until his death in 1897.

His hotel guests included the orator and abolitionist Frederick Douglass, but that didn't keep the newspapers of the day from reporting on misdeeds and "misconduct" there.

It is not surprisingly, given the prominent "Uptown" locations of Spence's Restaurant, and Burns' Great Oyster House, they too faced major legal struggles. In Spence's case, he had brushes with the law years before he embarked in business with his father, Henry Spence, Sr. In 1874, James Spence (along with his brother, Henry) worked as a barber and moonlighted as a bartender for Patrick McCabe, an Irish man whose tavern may have been located on South Matlack Street. McCabe had fined on other occasions for providing minors with alcohol at his tavern, but the judge was said to have spared him a prison term because McCabe had lost his leg in a railroad accident. In 1874, Spence, however, was fined $100 and sentenced to 50 days in jail for thinking he could "give liquor to boys, corrupt their taste, and blight their hopes for their parents," as the court papers described it.

Around the same time, the East End's empty lots and pasture land were developed, and black-owned businesses began to disappear one by one from the center of town. Mysterious things happened: Hepburn had an altercation with an "obnoxious white stranger" at his hotel, resulting in his death in 1897. Fortune Fullerton was killed when he fell from a second-story window, leaving behind his family, a farm in West Bradford Township, a candy store and his oyster bar.

No investigation of a physical assault was made at the official inquest, although Hepburn was said to have suffered from "pulmonary problems." His untimely death at the age of 65 was unfortunate considering that he was seemingly finally free of legal entanglements: A grand jury had failed to indict him for "keeping a gambling house" and serving liquor "to a person of known intemperate habits."

Only a few accounts of Charles Burns' West Gay Street restaurant survive, though he was in business there for a quarter of a century. One account described his "escape" from the South with only his mother and two siblings. Born in Culpepper, Virginia in either 1855 or 1856, Burns suffered a childhood injury, or "terrible sear" on his face when the plantation mistress threw him against a fireplace grate. Accounts about his lifelong attempt to diversify his restaurant business, such as adding roasted peanuts, a bakery, a fruit stand, and ice cream to his offerings, were duly reported. But his forays into the laundry business and staging theatrical shows proved to be too foreign to him and were short-lived. His theater (its location is unknown) was in fact shut down for staging "bawdy" and half-nude productions.

Both James Spence and Burns were arrested during what could be described as the height of their businesses, in 1909 and 1908. Burns made no public statement but later appealed his $500 fine and three-month jail sentence to the state Supreme Court and lost. A few weeks before serving his sentence, Burns closed his restaurant where he had recently installed a soda fountain and a new steel range (said to be the largest in the

Left Inset: Moses G. Hepburn
Top Right: A c. 1908 birds-eye-view of West Chester as seen from the former steam plant at Chestnut and North Walnut Streets. Courtesy of William Supplee.

One of many tumble down buildings. Franklin near Market.

Dilapidated Tenement - 600 East Miner (front).

borough at the time) and had replaced the electric lights with stylish gas lights.

Interestingly, within a few years, in 1910, West Chester saw its peak in the number of black residents – 2,500 – and the black business community had grown so much, it earned its own chapter in a statewide directory of "Negro Businesses." Many of the would-be restaurant owners worked in catering and others were small-scale business owners such as Orlando Cummings, who taught music on East Market Street and Jessie Kelley, who had an "Express" and grocery at 154 West Gay.

As the book's "Uptown" map reveals, black business in the early 20th and late 21st century tended to be clustered together. Many saw a succession of black owners.

In a 1995 *Philadelphia Inquirer* story, the late Gertrude "Trudy" Ferguson recalled the many enterprises of her father's, including the Royal Palace (now the Star Social Club). The place "hopped" with dance bands and jazz ensembles in the 1940s and '50s.

The late Warren Burton, then 91, recalled a more refined West Chester, when there were many small but thriving businesses, such as the tenor who taught music lessons on Adams Street. He recalled the years when residents could buy seafood at a black-run business on the corner of Market and Matlack Streets, or see pyramids of fruit and vegetables displayed outdoors at an Italian market at New and Gay Streets.

Warner Durnell, who was 75 in 1995 and still running his venetian blind-cleaning business, recalled that many blacks who didn't have their own businesses found work in the local brickyards, or "The Yard," as the area south of Union Street and east of Adams Street was called. Fittingly, the bricks they made at "The Yard" were often used to build community structures such as the Bethel AME Church.

Residents interviewed about West Chester's black community during the Civil Rights era, naturally recalled Bayard Rustin. Although Rustin is best known for his work as special assistant to the Rev. Dr. Martin Luther King Jr. and for organizing the historic 1963 march on

Washington, D.C., residents generally remembered him for his early efforts to shake up the sleepy town of West Chester, where despite its Quaker heritage and early black community, prejudices ran so deep that, the town was dubbed "Little Mississippi" in the 1960s.

It was here that Rustin, who grew up with his grandparents in a series of rented houses, became a Quaker and began to practice a non-violent type of civil rights activism that he later shared with King. Even as a high school student, Rustin would try to get his friends to take part in "sit-ins" at West Chester restaurants. In his senior year, he was arrested for attempting to sit in the "white section" of the old Warner movie theater on High Street.

Years later, in the mid-1960s, Rustin returned home, interrupting his work on national civil rights issues to help launch a drive to end segregation and job discrimination in the local schools. Under his leadership, "Mr. March" encouraged local residents to form a fair housing demonstration in 1966, and to picket the local banks to persuade them to hire blacks – a campaign that was ultimately successful. As the local businesswoman Alice M. Thomas, who co-owns an antique shop on Church Street, once said of Rustin, "He never forgot his friends. He always came back."

Curiously, the controversy occasioned by Rustin's past critics – those who cited him as gay, black or Communist – did not die with him. In 2003, sixteen years after his death, it took a series of acrimonious public debates before the West Chester District Area school board decided to name a new high school, the Bayard T. Rustin Memorial High.

Bayard M. Rustin Courtesy of CCHS

A band preforming an operetta at the West Chester Community Center, now the Melton Center. Courtesy of CCHS

The Community

The following was written by W.T.M. Johnson in 1998 at the request of Sarah Wesley, who was preparing an early version of this walking tour. It was titled "The West Chester Three."

When I think of walking through West Chester, Pennsylvania, I think of three African American young men who walked through West Chester some 60 years ago. They were friends, about the same age, who faced and fought racism, the daily bread of all African Americans. And they each "overcame" – at least as much as any African American. The three were Charles Melton, Charles Porter, and Bayard Rustin. They grew up together, socialized together, played sports together, they were friends all their lives. But each was a strong-willed, complex individual. Charles Melton was quick to fight, a scrapper. Charles Porter was slower to take offense, but just as much a fighter as Charles Melton. Bayard Rustin was the pacifist,

non-violent, possibly because of his Quaker upbringing, but he was just as unyielding in his beliefs. Three strong-willed men.

All three played sports, and all were members of the 1931 championship football team. Look at the picture in Henderson High School. Charles Porter told me about a football practice session that was attended by his mother. The trouble started when the coach kicked Charles Porter for some reason. Charles said his mother came out of the stands with her pocketbook swinging against the coach's head. She told him never to do that again to her son. I don't think he ever did. And Charles Porter told me that on a track team trip to Altoona, he and Bayard, the two African American members of the team, were told they could not stay at the hotel with the rest of the team. They told the coach, "No rooms, no running." They got rooms

They told the coach, "No rooms, no running." They got rooms.

1: Paul Hill **2**: Eddie Richardson, Alfred Boydl, Gene Allen **3**: Ernest Irons & friend **4**: Children at the Community Center **5**: Silver Melton, Regina Williams Charlotte Lee **6**: Dot Jackson's lawn party behind her W. Gay Street home **7**: John & Julia Clark **8**: The Community Bar

He helped establish an organization of African American Artists in West Chester.

Charles Melton became associated with the West Chester Community Center, an association that was to last 42 years. He was "Mr. Everything." He did it all: he led the picketing of the banks to force them to hire African Americans as something besides janitors. He also led protests against racism in the schools. He helped win a lawsuit against Lukens Steel, and he helped change the election system in West Chester—just before he died in 1987.

Charles Porter was also a "Mr. Everything." He was, perhaps, the most extravagantly talented of the three; he did many things, all of them very well. He was a painter, sculptor, musician, iron worker, stone mason, and animal trainer. He helped establish an organization of African American Artists in West Chester. In his later life, he moved to New Hope and was very much at home in that arts colony. His jazz parties were well-attended and great fun.

Bayard Rustin's path is well-known: pacifist, non-violent protester, freedom fighter, lecturer, organizer and planner. He provided

crucial assistance to Dr. Martin Luther King, Jr. in the Civil Rights struggle and also to A. Philip Randolph in planning and carrying out the historic 1963 March on Washington.

All three were equally great men. All made the world a fairer, better place. I have a mental picture of all of them standing together, smiling. The occasion was the dedication of the annex to the West Chester Community Center in May 1975. Charles Porter died later in 1993. At his funeral in West Chester, a group of his musician friends played a tune at his graveside. They had an acoustic bass, clarinet, and flute. The tune they played was a perfect description of Charles Porter, but it also perfectly fit the other two of the West Chester Three: "Unforgettable."

All three were equally great men. All made the world a fairer, better place.

1: W.T. M. Johnson **2**: A class posing in front of the Gay Street School **3**: Olive Ringgold and Jane Hill **4**: The West Chester Community Center, now The Melton Center **5**: In front, Jason Medley and sister Leslie **6**: The Spriggs familyat play behind the Star Social

Charles A. Melton Arts and Education Center

501 East Miner Street

GETTING THERE:
The center is located on East Miner Street, between South Adams and South Worthington Street. Parking is available at the center's lot off East Market.

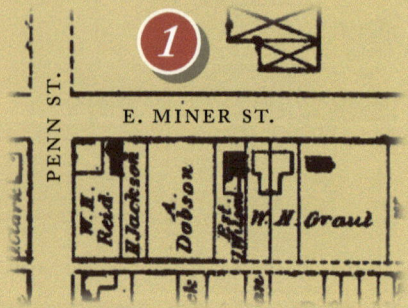

Bayard Rustin's grandparents, Julia and Janifer Rustin, were founding members of the center as well the Chester County branch of the NAACP.

Formerly known as the West Chester Community Center, this site has long and distinguished record of serving the social, educational, and recreational needs of the town's African American population. Many credit Cheyney educator, Dr. Leslie Pickney Hill, for encouraging residents to establish the center in 1919. In interviews, Hill often cited his motivations for the center's founding. Early in his career as president of what was then Cheyney Training School for Teachers, Hill noticed a sign posted in a West Chester park that read, "No Dogs Allowed. No Negroes Allowed." Dismayed by this, Dr. Hill realized that there was a real need for a place where facilities could be used on a nondiscriminatory basis.

Hill was familiar with West Chester because many Cheyney students came here to teach extracurricular courses in sewing, cooking, Bible study, and carpentry in the basement of the Gay Street School. He began there to formulate his ideas and reach out to the community. He spoke to groups at places such as the Bethel A.M.E. Church and proposed that a community house be constructed to assist in such aspects as character development within the African-American community and to aid in interracial cooperation.

One early idea included an unique strategy to interest the community in his plans: he proposed sending 300 letters to African American residents and 1,000 letters to white potential supporters. In time, Hill would realize his dreams of an interracial fraternity. When the board of trustees was founded in 1919, it was one of the first interracial boards in Pennsylvania.

Some highlights of the center:

In the summer of 1945, Bayard Rustin attended the first planning meeting for the Committee of Racial Understanding at the center. Perhaps the most interesting activity of the group was to send a series of so-called "testers" to area restaurants, who then wrote reports on whether black members were served any differently than the organization's white members.

In 1965, Rustin again returned to the center, interrupting his work on national civil rights issues to help launch a drive to end segregation and job discrimination in the local schools. He also returned in the mid-1960s to help organize fair housing protests in West Chester and to picket the local banks, persuading them to hire blacks. All the protesters had their meetings at the center.

In 1946, an athletic field was dedicated in honor of residents who had served in World War II. In 1950, the swimming pool was built. It was later dedicated to community activist Norman Bond. A large room used as a multi-purpose room was named in honor of Charles A. Melton, a well-known activist and executive director of the center from 1966 to 1980.

On August 14, 2004, a formal ceremony took place to honor and pay tribute to Melton and the center was renamed the Charles A. Melton Arts and Education Center.

Facing page: The center today.
Above Photo collage: Clifford E. DeBaptiste takes a turn with the shovel at the 1975 groundsbreaking for the new annex. Warren Burton (lt.) and Charles Swope (rt) are also pictured.

The original center, built 1934.

When the building was completed in 1934, it contained a large auditorium, offices, a furnished library (later named for Dr. Hill) and a small kitchen.

Around the Neighborhood

400-500 Block
of East Miner Street

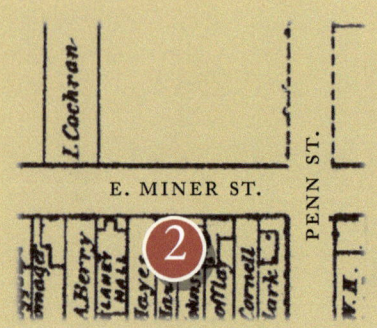

When the community center acquired its property here in 1917, the land overlooked a large ice pond and had long been called the "Drover's lot." A 1915 sales notice described it as including brick and frame stables, livestock yards and pig pens.

On an 1883 map, Penn Street ran down to East Market, with pasture land on either side belonging to I.S. Cochran, who owed a large livery stable on East Market and had a busy trade with drovers, who drove livestock to Philadelphia. The East End landlord, John George owned a lot at what is now the playing grounds of the center, which he never developed.

George was one of West Chester's wealthiest citizens and had property lots throughout the East End. He once explained his holdings as being for the "colored folks of the borough" who were "having a rather serious time in securing residences and were being driven from place to place." In the mid-1800s, however, George's real estate dealings with black residents was bitterly denounced by the editor of the *American Republican*. The editor, George Pearce, accused George of "colonization" – creating a warren of the worst elements of poor and black communities.

Abram Dobson, an early black journalist, owned property directly across from the community center. He considered real estate to be the path to financial and spiritual freedom. And while he often rented his properties to fellow black residents, his East Miner Street property was never developed, judging from early maps. It remains an open lot today.

Water-loving sycamores grow here, a reminder of the former ice pond.

St. Paul's Baptist Church

418 East Miner Street (original site, now Highway Gospel)

This church had its beginnings in 1887 when a group gathered at a house on East Market for what was termed a meeting of "The Baptist Colored Mission." The church today is considered to be the oldest Baptist Church of African American heritage in the area.

The original church at the present site was vastly altered in the 1970s. However its original stain glass windows can still be seen. Early photographs of the church show its massive steeple and a steep flight of stone steps leading to a pair of beautifully carved doors with a stain glass arch overhead.

The property was purchased in 1893 and a church built soon after. However, within a few years, in 1898, the congregation suffered a blow. The church hall burned, and services had to be held for nearly a year at the nearby Adams Street School. The church was rebuilt in 1899 and by 1916, the church was thriving with membership totaling 200, a new $4,200 organ, and new church parsonage at 252 East Gay.

Again misfortune struck the church building, this time in the form of lightning in 1936. Services were held at the Second Presbyterian Church. The church moved in the 1980s to its present location, then a former hardware store, where the congregation had to make do without pews and even meeting rooms. Today, their church is completely renovated and their old church now houses the Highway Gospel Community Temple.

Above: The original stain glass windows can still be seen today.
Inset: An undated photo of St. Paul's on East Miner. Courtesy St. Paul's.

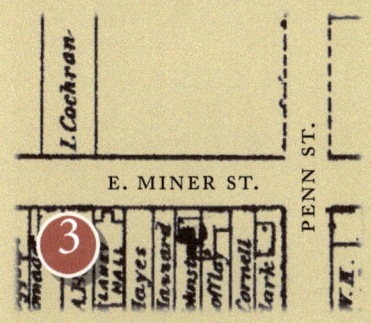

The lot on Miner Street was purchased from Thomas E. Wesley for $300.

Bethel A.M.E. Church

334 East Miner Street

GETTING THERE:
The Bethel A.M.E. Church is located on the south side of East Miner, about midway between South Adams and South Franklin.

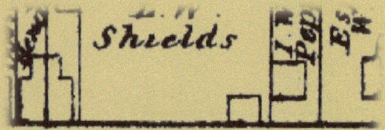

E. MINER ST.

This A.M.E. church was said to be the first church for African Americans in West Chester.

The church's first location.

This A.M.E. church was said to be the first church for African Americans in West Chester. However, its congregation did not have a building of its own for a generation after its founding in 1816. Initially, members met in a residence on West Gay Street. In 1834, a five-acre tract was purchased on West Miner Street (Everhart Grove) and the church that was built was known as the Zion A.M.E. Church. The first ministers on record were two brothers, Thomas and William Henry. The church was dedicated in 1830 when Reverend Israel Scott was pastor. They worshipped in this building until the beginning of the Civil War, then they moved to a rented building at the corner of Barnard and Adams Streets. In 1861, Old Zion was sold and after attempting to build elsewhere, the congregation decided to build here, changing the name of the church to Bethel in the process. The construction of the present church building was said to have been greatly aided by Moses Hepburn, West Chester's first black councilman. At the time, Hepburn owned several properties including the Magnolia Hotel and a house and lot across the street.

Above: Founded in 1816, the church today remains traditional in its style of worship.

The Bethel congregration, circa 1880. Photo courtesy of CCHS

He used his properties as collateral to purchase bricks from the A.D. Sharpless brickyard.

Early newspaper items about the Bethel Church reveal its lively community life. Entertainments included "cake walks" led by the Liberty Cornet Band and choir presentations led by A.J. Darnell. Many community meetings took place at the church. Two meetings in 1880 concerned the lack of black teachers at the Adams Street School, and the presentation of a banner made by the ladies of the church to the members of the "colored" Masonic order.

Right: Note the elaborate carpentry work at Bethel's parsonage.

Rice's Temple A.U.M.P. Church

326 East Miner Street
(original site)

GETTING THERE:
Rice's Temple is away from Franklin, next door to Bethel (#3).

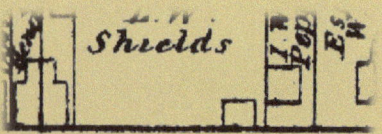

Mrs. Mattie Raymond suggested that the name of the church be changed to "Rice's Temple," which was approved unanimously.

This church had its beginnings on June 27, 1935, when a meeting was held at the home of Mrs. Mattie Raymond, at 217 North New Street. There were more than twenty members in attendance, and Bishop Rice informed them that he had been able to secure the Masonic Hall, at 326 East Miner Street, as a place to worship with the understanding that the Masons would retain the third floor area for their meeting room. The rental fee would be $6.00 per month. Bishop Rice named the church The Community Union Methodist Church.

Finally, in 1943, the church was able to purchase the building and the lot they had rented for some time. They bought it from Harry F. Taylor for $1,600, and the building included three ground-floor apartments. For extra income, they also rented the third floor to the Masons.

On Sunday, July 25, 1945, the church had its Mortgage Burning Service and Mrs. Mattie Raymond suggested that the name of the church be changed to "Rice's Temple," which was approved unanimously.

In 1967, Rice's Temple purchased the present property at 236 E. Gay Street, which was the former Church of Ascension of the Episcopal Diocese.

Above: Rice's congregation posed in front of the Mason Lodge on East Miner, Sept. 5, 1948. Photo by the former Belt's Studio. Courtesy of CCHS. Inset: The congregation in front of the present-day church. Photo courtesy of Harry Parrish.

The "Yard"
300 Block of East Miner

For decades beginning in the 1930s, a large expanse of land along Miner Street extending to Market street was occupied by Harman's junkyard. Its size and standing as business was reflected in the fact that "Harmon's Junkyard" appeared on borough maps at the time. Theodore Harmon originally had a lot along South Franklin street (once owned by Moses Hepburn), parallel to the present-day Rubensteins, but he later moved to this location where his son continued the business through the 1960s. The "Yard" is still remembered by many in the East End.

Early photos show the yard as bordering a small creek known as the Goose Creek, which led to a large commercial ice pond on East Market. In the 1900s, when the majority of African-Americans in West Chester lived in East End, the Goose Creek was known as "Shallow Run" on insurance runs. Goose Creek is a feeder creek to the Chester Creek, one of Chester County's most scenic streams. However, in the 19th century, this stretch of water served as a sewer for the southeast section of the borough.

In the late 1880s, improving the East Ward must have been a key priority for newly elected Borough Councilman Moses Hepburn. One notice, in 1882, announced that P.J. Barry began "turn-piking" Miner Street from the railroad to "Mr. Hepburn's Magnolia House Hotel." Another notice in 1884, indicates that they were still working on the project, placing stone curbing "on both sides" of East Miner Street, between Franklin and Adams.

Above: The "Yard." Photo courtesy of Helen Betty Ringgold.

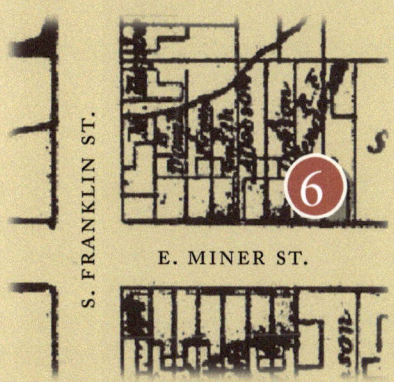

Harmon's "Junkyard" was once occupied by L.W. Shields' plaster and building supplies.

Nathan Holmes Post, American Legion #362

301 East Miner Street, corner of Franklin (site demolished)

The Nathan Holmes Post, circa 1908, CCHS, *(left) and as it appears it in 1995.* Photo by T. Mark Cole.

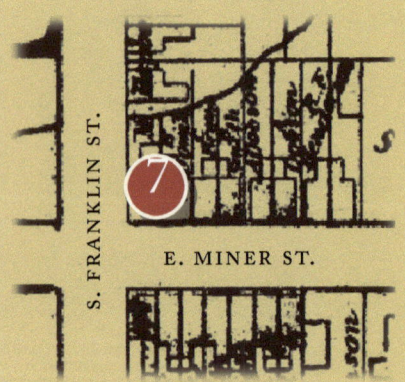

Most significant was its years as the site of West Chester's first African-American Legion.

For decades a massive brick Victorian with a mansard roof stood at the corner and served the community in different ways. Most significant was its years as the site of West Chester's first African-American American Legion. Known as the Nathan Holmes Post, American Legion #362, the lodge was founded in 1919 with thirteen charter members. The post was named in honor of a West Chester veteran of the First World War who was killed in action. For many years, the post rented the third floor of the present site, but following World War II, when the group saw a surge in membership, the post had numerous building drives in hopes of finding a new location. (See site #29) Eventually, the post acquired the entire building here.

In the late 1920s and 30s, members included Horace Pippin. He had not been discovered as America's greatest "primitive" artist but one of his assignments, as vice-president commander, was to oversee the making of the "marching squad" uniforms in 1929. Pippin, who had served in the all-black 369th U.S. Infantry, later became commander of the post. He was said to have never missed any local patriotic events and proudly wore his Purple Heart when it was belatedly awarded him in 1945.

In the 1940s and late '50s, the site was another community landmark – the corner building housed "Hunks" Restaurant, owned and operated by Hunk Johnson and James and Nancy Gallimore. They were known for their delicious meals and "subs" and had a thriving business. Then Hunks moved to East Market Street and this building became a private residence.

Left: A glimpse of the former George house, extreme left in this 1925 photo. Courtesy Hagley Library.

Above: The row of houses behind the little girl were once occupied by Rice's Temple.

John George's House

Corner of East Market & South Franklin Street (site demolished)

GETTING THERE:
The house was demolished. The former lot is now a parking lot next to Rubinstein's, at South Franklin and East Market.

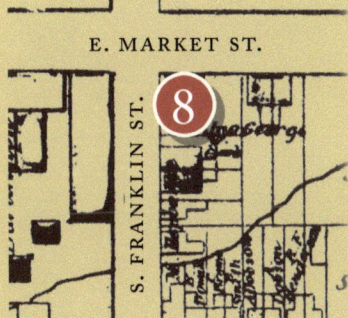

Sometime after 1849 the abolitionist John George built a house on the corner of East Market and South Franklin. The house was then in what was considered woodland, far from outskirts of West Chester. It is not known if George had planned to live in the house, since he soon rented it to a black laborer named Henry Robinson.

A few years later, Robinson managed to purchase a lot next door for $12, building what was described as a "cabin" on the lot. Abram Dobson and Moses G. Hepburn also owned houses and lots in the block. Dobson and Hepburn, in fact, had several landholdings in the East End that would soon exceed George's, and that helped them become influential figures in the black and white communities.

Although George's house was torn down, it is one of the few documented stations on the Underground Railroad. George was assisted by only a handful of local Quakers including Samuel M. Painter, a bookseller (See #9 on the Uptown tour.) Apparently, George's association with the black community made it easier to ask for assistance, but it is Painter's obituary that credits the help of three black residents, Abraham Shadd, Benjamin Freeman, and John Brown. Nineteenth-century newspaper accounts have reported that as many as 16 runaways were hidden in George's house, and that George armed many of his black tenants with old-time shot pistols in case bounty hunters came knocking on their doors. One reporter recalled that "the runaways were always directed at this house as a safe refuge, it being described to them as the house with seven stairs and full of windows."

The runaways were always directed to this house as a safe refuge.

The Magnolia House

300 East Miner

GETTING THERE: The Magnolia House is closed to the public but can be seen on the corner of South Franklin and East Miner.

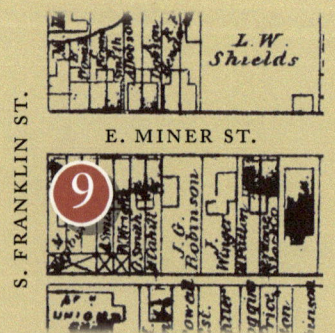

A sales notice of the Magnolia House hints of its large size for the times: "For sale: A three-story brick building, containing nineteen rooms, well-furnished and in good condition, and stabling for fifteen horses."

This corner location, which still operates as a boarding house, may be one of the East End's most celebrated sites.

The 19-room Magnolia House stood on the fringes, but thrived for more than a half-century beginning in 1866. That was when an entrepreneur named Moses G. Hepburn obtained his hotel license with the help of a West Chester judge, John Hickman, a former congressman and state legislator who was an early advocate of civil rights.

Hepburn was described in 1897 as the "wealthiest and best-known colored man in Chester County."

He built his brick hotel in 1860 and welcomed all "permanent and transient boarders," as one reporter put it in 1892, but was best known for hosting "prominent colored personages." One reporter recalled the time when, around 1880, Frederick Douglass "registered at the Magnolia House and expressed himself quite pleased to find such a fine hotel for the accommodation of the colored race."

Historian Robert Bussel writes of Hepburn's "ongoing contact" with such people as Douglass, "the journalist William Howard Day and visiting members of the black clergy," who all helped him prepare for what was

Above: Front view of the former hotel. Above (Left): A Rear view of the hotel today. (Right): A community store stood next door.

described as a "leadership role" within the black community. That included serving as the borough's first black councilman in 1882.

Hepburn operated the Magnolia House for 30 years until his untimely death at the age of 65 years, on the night of December 1, 1897. It is believed that he was living at the time across the street, at 331 East Miner. One paper described his death as being a bit "strange," having been witnessed by his "dear friends, Capt. Levi Hood, Solomon Hazard, and Nathan Priggs."

The account was as follows: "That day two strange white men came into the hotel. There were words between Mr. Hepburn and one of the strangers. Mr. Hepburn staggered back into the living room and died." There were "no wounds," the account noted.

On December 6, 1897, Hepburn was laid out, "clad in the uniform of a Knight Templar and with the hat and sword of the order reposing on the cloth-covered coffin," [decorated] with engraved Masonic marks and emblems." There were 12 pallbearers, six of whom were fellow members of the Masonic order; the other six friends included James Spence, Levi Hood, and Solomon Hazard. Soon after, Hepburn's son-in-law, John Wesley Smothers, took over the hotel and managed it for several more decades.

When Hepburn's widow, Christiana, died on September 9, 1921 ("about" the age of 85), her obit noted that the family had "amassed a confortable fortune in the hotel business."

Moses G. Hepburn

Hepburn was described in 1897 as the "wealthiest and best-known colored man in Chester County."

Hoopes Brothers & Darlington Wheel Works

Corner of South Franklin and East Market to Union (site demolished)

GETTING THERE:
None of the original buildings still stand but the main "spoke turning" and "sawing and planing" took place on the site now occupied by Rubinsteins' and the Salvation Army on East Market.

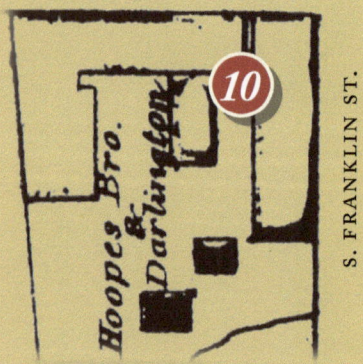

Hoopes was once the borough's largest enterprise.

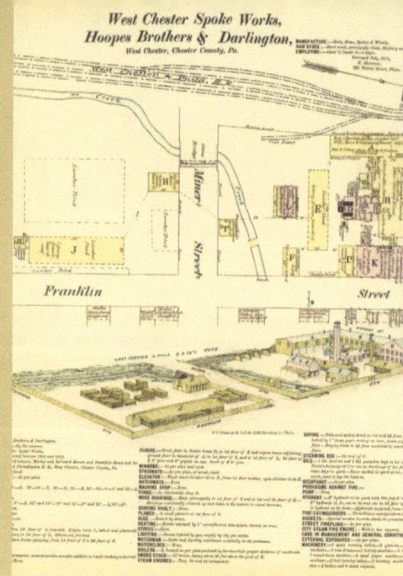

Considering the East End's early abundance of lumber yards and its access to the railroad, it is not surprising that a firm that especially relied on an abundance of wood would be established here. This was the firm of Hoopes Bro. & Darlington, a wheel and spoke manufacturer that exemplified the progressive times. The firm was founded in 1866 by two brothers, Thomas and William Hoopes, who made wheel spokes on their farm near West Chester. Within a year, the brothers moved their business to this location and launched a course of development that kept pace with any enterprise of the day.

At the height of production in the 1880s, the brothers (who later acquired a partner) employed 150 to 200 men and was making 45,000 sets of wheels on steam-operated machines. Its products were mass-produced and sold on a national and international scale. The company supplied Conestoga wagon wheels to the U.S. Army, and light carriage wheels to England. In 1870, according to one newspaper, Hoopes supplied a French firm with the wheel parts for "a coach for Emperor Napoleon." Eventually

Above: The Hexamer Survey of 1879 was used for insurance purposes, outlining production and safety features. Hoopes Spokes Works had fire buckets and a night and day watchmen but no lighting rods. The survey noted that an "underground passage" was located under Miner Street.

This early photo shows the extensive operations of Hoopes Bros. & Darlington Wheel Works as seen from Market Street. Note the access to the Pennsylvania Railroad. Photo Courtesy of CCHS.

the "Spokes Works," as they were commonly called, became West Chester's largest industrial enterprises and one of its largest employers. Amazingly, it continued to produce wheels (used as lamps) until it closed in 1973.

During a slow period in the 1950s, when the demand for wheels dropped, many of the buildings along Franklin Street were leased. One of the business that leased several buildings also became known as the most notorious place to work in black community – Nachman Spring Company. Many black residents today recall when the Nachman's became the focus of community attention and what historian Jim Jones calls "a strenuous attempt to organize labor" in the late 1950s. Jones writes that "on the second try in 1958, Nachman employees voted to join the United Steel Workers. However, four years later they voted to leave the union and the company quickly fired eleven local officers. The fired employees sued and won what has been termed the largest settlement made under the [orders of] the National Labor Relations Board.

Facing page: An interior view of Hoopes. Courtesy of CCHS.
Right: This early ad shows the third partner Edward S. Darlington. Courtesy of William Supplee.

Around the Neighborhood
200 Block
of East Market Street

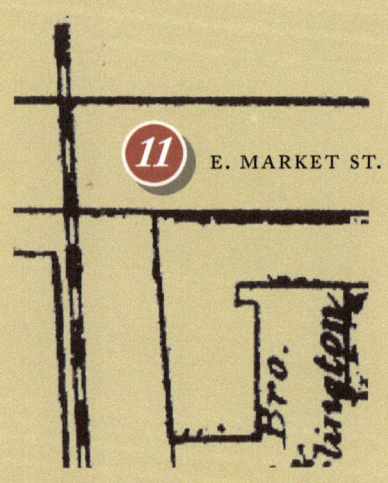

This block includes the home of George Wesley Blount, a celebrated black author and journalist.

What did this neighborhood look like in the days of the omnibus? In 1870, one news item, published after a major fire destroyed six homes at the corner of Market and Franklin, had the headline: "Georgetown: How Negroes Live in West Chester." The homes, one of which formerly housed a black-owned printing business, were described as being built of "fragments of old buildings torn down in other sections of the borough and put into shape there for the accommodation of (whoever) was willing to occupy them at exorbitant rates. These were miserable shanties… rented for $5 to $7 per room per month."

On the north side of Market Street, there are several buildings of interest. One of the three houses that now stands directly across from Rubinsteins was the home of George Wesley Blount, an author, journalist, and as he described himself in his newspaper columns, a "freedom Speaker." Blount was so outspoken for his time, his pithy sayings were dubbed "blountisms." Blount, who was born on January 29, 1879 in North Carolina, came to West Chester in 1927. During World War I, he promoted patriotism in his newspaper columns and received many awards for his editorial work and his skills as a speaker.

Blount worked as the director of the public relations department at Cheyney State Teachers College (now university). In his free time, he began to write editorials on his observations on everyday life, and as one columnist friend put it, "how the human race ticks." Blount received special recognition for those editorials concerning civil rights and personal rights, such as the right of free speech. In the 1950s, he was honored four times by the Freedom Foundation in Valley Forge. Later, when his book, *Observation of Life.* was published, he received endorsements from prominent political leaders, including then vice-president Richard M. Nixon.

Ralph G. Smith (now closed)

239 East Market Street

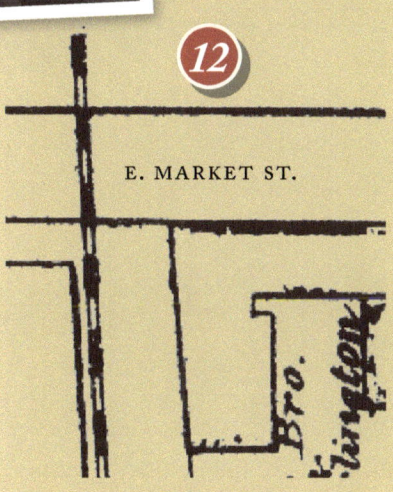

Although the building is now obscured by siding, this once stately brick building housed the former offices of Hoopes Spokes Works. A hint of the elaborate brickwork used throughout the Hoopes complex can perhaps be best seen in the chimney of this building. Today, the building is best associated with the Ralph Smith moving company, which had its offices and warehouse here.

Known for his enterprise, Ralph G. Smith Sr. had hauling in his blood stream. His father Gunkle W. Smith hauled goods by horse and wagon and a great grandfather had a horse-drawn taxi service. Eventually, the business encompassed general freight and warehousing, but it was best known for its horse transportation. Once described as the oldest horse hauling business in the nation, Ralph G. Smith hauled the likes of Sea Biscuit and War Admiral. At the time, the business was also located in Lexington, Kentucky and used state-of-the-art horse trailers. One 1939 van was featured in the *Daily Local News* after it was "retired" in 1959. Son Ralph Smith Jr., who took over the company in 1942, had planned to donate the van to a museum but it was destroyed by fire when arsonists attacked the company's equipment sheds at Linden and South Franklin Streets in the 1980s. That was one downturn in otherwise successful business. Two of Ralph Smith Jr.'s four sons were involved in the business at this location until recently.

Above left: Notice the original carved doors and wainscoting. Right: A turn-of-the-century photo of Gunkle W. Smith & Sons. Courtesy of William Supplee. Inset: The elegant chimney dates to 1867 when the building served as the office of Hoopes Spokes Works.

This business once hired early black workers as "haulers" and stable men.

The West Chester Rail Station

200 Block
of East Market Street
(site demolished)

GETTING THERE:
The former Market Street station was demolished, but a small station used for a tourist railroad now stands near the railroad tracks between South Matlack and South Franklin. Weekend scenic train rides can be taken.

The original station house was two stories when it was built in 1867.

This site has been partly preserved by the West Chester Railroad Heritage Association, an all-volunteer, non-profit corporation that operates a tourist railroad here.

Despite a major fire in 1885, the former massive rail station, complete with Palladian windows and protective eaves, remained relatively unchanged from 1885 to 1968. Its demolition in June, 1968 was a major architectural loss to the borough.

After the fire in 1885, the local newspaper reported that many improvements were being made to the depot including the installation of new gas lamps and "air" vents as well as galvanized screens in the waiting rooms. Other improvements to the station, which one reporter described as being "fitted up in a grand style," included steam heat and the addition of a third floor. An inscription was set above the main door that read: West Chester & Philadelphia RR Depot Via Media. The passenger shelter was also equipped with new electric lights in 1886.

At its peak in the 1920s, the depot handled about 6,000 passengers a day, but by the time it closed in 1965, ridership had declined to a weekly average of 320 people, mainly because of poor service and poor management of the line, according to historian Jim Jones.

Above: The former passenger shelter, circa 1960. Passengers in the mid-1980s faced poor service, partly because of major delays and SEPTA required Philadelphia-bound passengers to take a bus first to the town of Elwyn. Above inset: The Market Street Station as it looked in the late 1950s. Photo from the Ned Goode collection. CCHS

The Rail Yards

(now occupied by WCRHA)

E. MINER ST.

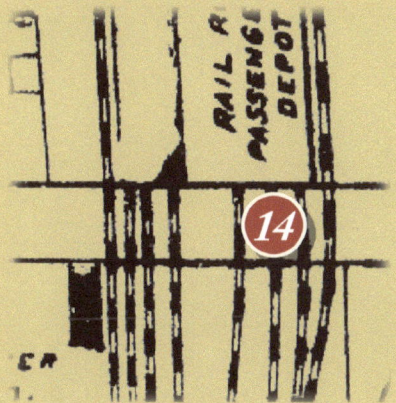

For almost a decade, after 1833, there were actually two rail lines in West Chester – one came from Malvern, and another took passengers to West Philadelphia via the town of Media. In 1867, the two lines were combined and the Market Station was built.

The rail yards were built on land acquired by the railroad in 1852. By 1891, a three-story station stood in the middle of a network of rail lines that included three freight lines and two passengers lines. Additional rail lines continued past Market Street to another terminus on East Biddle street. There also was a special freight line that went into a siding to serve the Hoopes Spoke Works and cattle pens southeast of the Market Street station.

In recent years, the rail yards were shared by the Pennsylvania Railroad and SEPTA, which launched a passenger express direct to Philadelphia in 1966. The service was discontinued in the mid-1980s.

In early photographs, a towering water tank appears next to the PRR rail station, advertising the "West Chester Wheel Works, Hoopes Bros. and Darlington."

The rail yards were built on land acquired by the railroad in 1852.

Around the Neighborhood

100 Block
of East Market Street

GETTING THERE:
The neighborhood of the 100 block of East Market is best visited on foot. The closest public parking is on East Gay, between High and South Matlack.

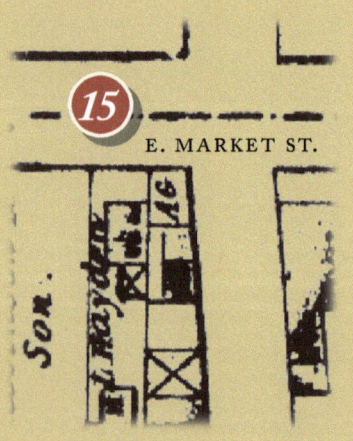

As one progresses up East Market Street, one sees the several original Civil War-era row houses. These buildings were built following the completion of West Chester's second rail line in 1858. Even before that, the entire area was an industrial site that included greenhouses, a coal storage place run by Darlington & Williams, and stables owned by Isaac Cochran. Another large stable operation, Thomas McLaughlin, stood at 114-116 East Market. In 1906, McLaughlin advertised a livery, feed, and boarding stable here. He also had a veterinarian on the premises who had an appropriate name, Charlie Oat.

In the midst of these enterprises, there were several black-owned businesses. On the north side of East Market, at 220, stood Oscar Ray's grocery store. A few doors up was another neighborhood grocery, the American Store. At the red brick building top right, Sarah Spangler ran a small restaurant where Horace Pippin once displayed his work and was soon "discovered" as an artist. In the early 1960s, #211 East Market housed "J.J's" Restaurant, owned and operated by Grace and Arthur Jones. There was also "Hunks" Restaurant, which relocated from East Miner (site #7) to 231 East Market Street sometime in the early 1960s.

The number of social venues and eateries here leads one to question the loss of community life in many small towns today. Going back to the 19th century, Moses Hepburn's will states that he left a "3 story store" and dwelling at 215 East Market. This would have been north of Market, on a lot bordering an alley and including a stable. Hepburn also owned what was described in the will as a "3 story brick dwelling on Market and Matlack," later the home of Harry "Hap's" Spriggs.

The Spriggs Family Home

Corner of East Market and North Matlack

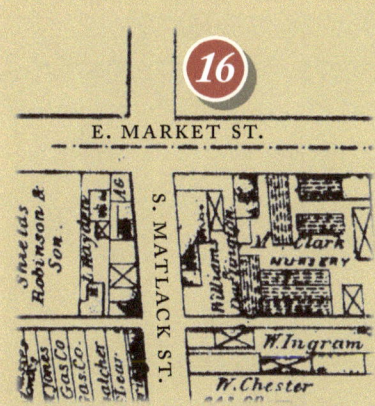

This site is best known as the long-time residence of the Spriggs family. The house, with its decorative paneled frieze, and carved cornice, was built by an early physician named C.L. Kelling. He advertised that he could cure "cancer and other chronic diseases" and lived conveniently near the rail depot. Known as the Cancer Institute of West Chester, Kelling had a second location, where he sold patented medicines, and his own potions, on West Gay Street.

Kelling died in 1870 and his estate didn't sell his house until 1895, when it was acquired by Moses G. Hepburn. Of all the black entrepreneurs, Hepburn had an unusual career path. Not only did he enter politics, He was born and raised in Alexandria, Virginia but studied in the West Chester's Quaker schools. His father, also named Moses, was a slave who had been "liberated by his [white] paternal parent." Since children of slaves could not be educated in Virginia schools, Hepburn Senior sent his son north to West Chester in 1818. Hepburn returned to the Alexandria, but despite his success running a "fishery" and supplying water to the city with "nine teams and nine men," he settled permanently in West Chester sometime in 1853. One of this first jobs was work as a barber at 6 East Market Street in 1857.

During the years Harry "Hap's" Sprigg lived in the house, this section of East Market was very busy place. Spriggs ran the "Royal Luncheonette" at 217 E. Market St, and within a few years purchased what was then a meeting place/farmers exchange called "P.J. McCormick's" (now the Star Social Club) and opened the "Royal Palace."

1: The former "Royal Luncheonette" at 217 E. Market Street. 2: Hap's Spriggs in the backyard of what is now the Star Social. Courtesy of CCHS. 3: The late Gertrude "Trudy" Spriggs Ferguson (L) with her sister. The Star Social can be seen in the background.

This site is best known as the long-time residence of the Spriggs family.

17

Star Social Club

212 East Market Street

GETTING THERE:
The Star Social Club is now a private club but can visited on the south side of E. Market, near the intersection of S. Matlack.

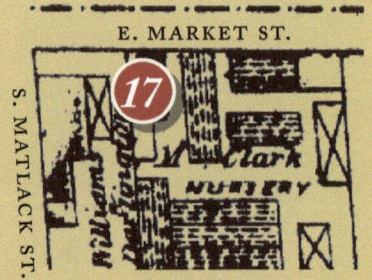

During its heyday, the Royal Palace (now the site of the Star Social Club) offered a range of entertainment from tenor soloists to big-name entertainers such as B.B. King and Duke Ellington.

The Star Social Club has been described as one the oldest black chartered organizations in the state, but the site also offers a mini history in the way organizations and community life has changed over the years. As with many early clubs, its founding members first met in private homes and rented rooms. The Star Social, however, had a particularly long period without a permanent home. It wasn't until 1953 that the cornerstone – amid a grand ceremony, complete with men in top hats – was laid in the building once known as "McCormick's Hall."

According to the club's written history, it originated in 1896 as a men's social club at the residence of Nelson Tyler, 319 Hannum Avenue, and was established "to promote activities and establish brotherhood among the Black community." At that time, the club was frequently referred to as the "Colored Social Club," and was cited as having only five members: James Edwards, John T. Melton, Willis Lampkins, George Whipper and Harry Berry. However, an early photograph shows eight men standing in front of sign that reads the Star Social Club.

Although the club's North Walnut location featured formal parlors and pool rooms, news items in the 1900s suggest that the club was not just another smoking den for card-and-pool-playing men. There were all-day outings at Deborah's Rock, a popular picnic spot along the Brandywine, as well as open-air dances and formal balls featuring "Prof. Jones' Orchestra."

In the 1940s and 1950s, the club continued to have a taste for refinement, inviting guest lecturers to speak and holding afternoon teas. At one point, after moving to its present site in the late 1950s, its walls were decorated with the murals of Horace Pippin.

More than a decade before the building housed the Star Social Club, it was a community center of musicians, friends, and families. They found everything they needed at the Royal Palace – music, food, and even maybe a bedroom set. Harry "Hap's" Spriggs displayed antiques and used furniture in the building's front window.

It was under Spriggs' management that the Royal Palace became the place for all generations, and for musicians, both famous and local. Leon Spriggs recalled that Friday night was a "big night," partly because the stores were open late, but also because the Palace accommodated so many with its auditorium, basketball court, dance stage, and even, at one point, a roller rink.

For music, the highlights included Count Basie and Fats Waller. Ray Charles did come to visit, but it was Sunday, and the Blue Laws were in effect. "He never played, he just had a drink or two," Leon Spriggs recalled.

1: Guests at the Star Social Club's annual anniversary dinner. Date unknown. **2**: The musicians include Herbert Steele (sitting) and Rob Irons with the instrument. **3**: The Masons officiated in the 1953 laying of the cornerstone in the newly renovated building. The stone building dates to the 1880s. **4**: The founders of the Star Social Club, circa 1896. **5 & 7**: The bar in the 1940s. **6**: The man in the Star Social cap is Benjamin Frederick Lampkins, Sr.

All photos courtesy of CCHS.

The Star Social Club today.

The Star Social Club has been described as one the oldest black chartered organizations in the state.

Capt. Levi M. Hood Lodge, #159

200 East Market Street

GETTING THERE:
The lodge is private but can be seen at the southwest corner of South Matlack and East Market.

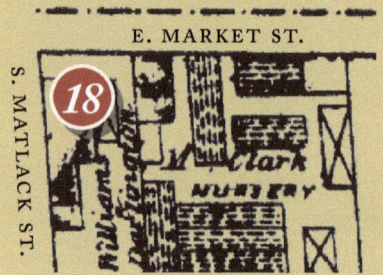

The Lodge was known as the "Colored Elks" in its early years.

Levi M. Hood

This early Elk's lodge was named for Levi M. Hood, who was a veteran of the "colored" troops during the Civil War and later earned his living as a shoemaker and as a bartender at the Magnolia House. The lodge was established in 1908 at a building at North Walnut Street, and the following year, was described by a local newspaper as "flourishing". Members were drawn not only from the immediate community, but from "Coatesville, Downingtown, Wayne, and Media," the paper reported, adding that "West Chester now has colored Masons, colored Odd Fellows, colored Knights of Pythias and colored Elks."

Early newspaper accounts suggest that Hood was active long before the lodge was founded. One news notice in 1871, for instance, read, "last week, commissioner Ingram organized a company of Negro soldiers in our borough. Levi M. Hood was elected Captain and turned out for the first time [in Coatesville's] Emancipation Celebration."

Throughout the 19th-century, lodge events often crossed all race barriers. There was an annual parade, for instance, held in September that drew

Above left: The Levi Hood Lodge was well known for its parades and patriotic displays. The band was formed sometime in 1914. The lodge renovated this c. 1880 building sometime in the 1920s.

many area Elks groups but was led by the Liberty Band, once described as the "best musical organization in the colored population of Philadelphia" area. In 1927, a woman's auxiliary was founded to help with fundraising and neighborhood projects. Local newspaper accounts were filled with their activities.

On the occasion of its 39th anniversary, in September of 1947, nearly 20 bands and drum and bugle corps turned out for the parade, marching from the community center (#1) through town to Wayne Street. By the 1940s and 1950s, the lodge's community activities included giving full-tuition college scholarships to young students. In May of 1954, the Lodge even sponsored a state-wide convention, which brought several days of speeches, lectures and community events, such as the first annual oratorical contest, state pageant and ball, and golfing rounds at Cobbs Creek Golf Course in Philadelphia.

After the lodge received its charter in 1908, it published its mission as open "only to American citizens of African descent." In addition to Walnut street, the lodge's former location include the Masonic lodge on East Miner and building on East Gay.

Above: Young marchers join in the annual Elks Parade, circa 1980 In the early 1900s, the Elks annual parade was led by the Liberty Cornet Band and nearly a hundred musicians from Philadelphia "colored" lodges. Photo by Sarah Wesley.
At right: The lodge featured an awning in the 1960s.
Below Right: The lodge in 1995. Photo by T. Mark Cole.

Around the Neighborhood

100 Block
of South Matlack Street

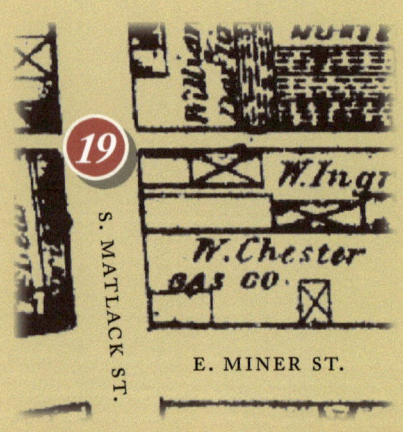

In the 1880s, this region was largely industrial.

In the 1880s, this region was largely industrial and (in some places) an undesirable place to live. In addition to noisy lumber, coal, and brick yards, the roads were often in need of repair due to the heavy traffic to and from the railroad and the West Chester Gas works. Judging from Boyd's Directory of the 1900s, (which listed occupations) South Matlack was home to laborers, butchers, shopkeepers, teachers, and waiters. There was also a mix of ethnic groups as well as black and white residents. For instance, William Hall, listed as a laborer, lived at # 20. A black carpenter, Henry Burns, (who may have been the son of restaurateur Charles H. Burns) resided at 17 South Matlack, adjacent to the gas works. Prior to that, 17 South Matlack was the longtime blacksmith shop of William Ingram, who was still shoeing horses through the early years of the automobile age. His stable stood on a narrow strip of land between the gas works and "Clark's" greenhouses. Other residents included many with Irish names such as Abram Berry, J. Farley, and James Finnegan,

Above: The former corner store as looks today, and below: Many veterans from World War II moved to the East End after the war.

who listed his occupation as a "wheeler," no doubt in reference to the Hoopes Spoke Works.

Other residents included many with Irish names such as Abram Berry, J. Farley, and James Finnegan, who listed his occupation as a "wheeler," no doubt in reference to the Hoopes Spoke Works.

For generations, many backyards in this neighborhood overlooked the railroad tracks. At the height of freight operations in 1891, freight trains rumbled through, carrying coal to the Gas Works and four coal yards. Freight cars also served the Spoke Works and Ralston Hoopes as well as the West Chester Ice Co. at East Union Street.

Top Left: A group of unknown bricklayers, some carrying brick hods, pose for the camera. For generations, West Chester's East End supplied the majority of the bricks used for new construction.

Top Right: An unidentified man stands on South Matlack. Cohen's corner store can be seen in the distance. Photo courtesy of John Clark.

Bottom: A view of the neighborhood as seen from the railroad tracks. Photo courtesy of John Clark.

Four sets of tracks went past the neighborhood.

The West Chester Gas Works

Corner of South Matlack and East Miner Streets (now the John O. Green Park)

This is now the site of the John O. Green Park.

For decades, the borough's main gas works were located at both the northeast and southeast corners of South Matlack and East Miner. Beginning in 1852 until it closed in the 1960s, the land was occupied by a very Oz-like brick building with a network of metal supports and tall chimneys spewing black smoke. The corner block north of this, bordering East Market Street, was lined by greenhouses owned by an Irish nurseryman named Michael Clark. His greenhouses were later destroyed by a gas works explosion (which sent bricks flying through the glass of the greenhouses) and Clark was forced to sell his business. He eventually settled into selling candy and flowers at a small stand inside the railroad depot.

No photos of the Gas Works have survived but based on similar gas works built to supply small towns with illuminating gas, the site had several coal yards. Coal was shoveled nearly around the clock and was heated by a series of boilers to extract the gas, which typically produced many hazardous by-products such as ammonia and hydrogen sulfide. Naturally, the gas works added an element of danger to the neighborhood. Indeed, the works blew up in more than one occasion.

In 1904, it was noted that "against the rules a night engineer, Charles Davis, entered the purifying dept of the plant" with a lantern. The "terrific"

Above: In addition to the Gas Works, the East End had several brick yards. Many black workers (the ones here all wearing hats) made their living at the "Yard."

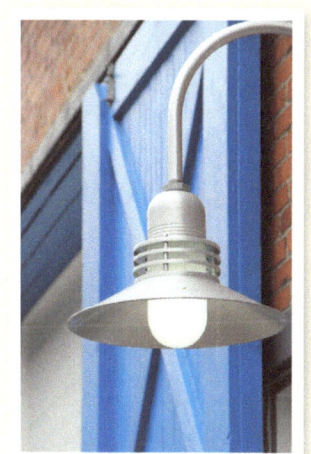

explosion caused a fire that raged for two hours and "rocked houses for several squares around." Among the damages: Patrick McCabe of South Matlack Street, where he had "long conducted a fine greenhouse in which he raised many grapes every season." Frozen hydrants hindered the fire fighters as they did in 1895, when a "colored" watchman, Joseph Bostick, "started the day, the regular watchman off duty because of small pox in his house."

Bostick carried no lamp, it was noted. The fire started when oil leaked out of the building.

A park now occupies the former gas works. It was donated to the borough by PECO and opened in 1999. Plans for the park began as early as 1996 when the site was bought for $1 from the owners at the time – the Philadelphia Electric Co. The park was to be named in honor of Horace Pippin, but when the former police chief, John O. Green, unexpectedly died in 1998, it was named for him. Green became West Chester's first black chief of police in the mid-1970s after he helped resolve a series of race riots in the borough.

Above left: A house along Cedar Alley, which once extended past the Gas Works and William Ingram's blacksmith shop. Photo by Cris Staley Hutchinson. The remains of several mechanic shops can be seen along the alley, including one with a hoist post which may have served the Shields, Robinson & Sons. Co. Lower right: East Miner Street showing the park in the distance.

21

East Miner Street

100 block
of East Miner Street

GETTING THERE:
This site is best reached by traveling down South Matlack from East Market, then making your first right onto East Miner. The house is on the north side, a few houses up from the intersection.

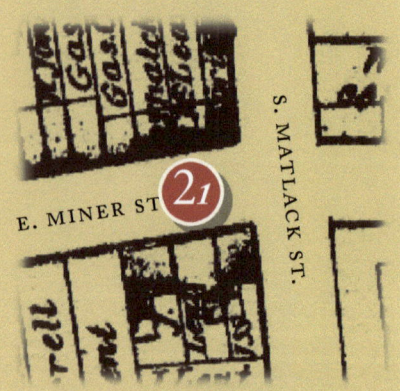

Barry's hauling business at 117 East Miner once had an empty lot next door.

Compared to other parts of East Miner street, this stretch was once considered a desirable place to live in the 19th century. For one thing, the houses were made of brick (not flimsy frame) and the area was also just above the flood plain of the Goose Creek. The occupants here included Patrick J. Barry, an industrious Irishman who operated a hauling business at 117 E. Miner Street. He was said to be one of two main builders and investors of Riggtown (see #12 on the industrial tour). Before he went into the construction business, he built a large trade by hauling goods to and from the railroad, gaining customers such as the Hoopes Spokes Works.

This street is of interest mainly because the dwellings were built to house working-class families. And yet they are fairly refined. Several of the houses in the low 20s and 30s have small third floor "attic" windows which is typical of Greek Revival and decorative touches that include brick "corbeling" or brackets under the eaves. Since the East End is known for its brick yards, it's not surprising that brick homes predominate. One exception: just north of the intersection of South Walnut Street, number 27 is one of only ten frame houses that pre-date the 1860s in West Chester. It has been described by architectural historian Jane Dorchester as a rare survivor of a frame dwelling that was typical of this area from 1840 to 1859.

It is not known if either James Spence or his brother Henry ever lived at 133 and 111 East Miner. But they were jointly taxed for the buildings in 1880, along with a "dwelling on an alley" behind #111. They are listed as "tavern keepers" in 1875, with only a lot and "shop" on East Miner.

James Spence, who was another southern transplant, was one of the founders of the Liberty Band comprised of members of the "colored" troops of the Civil War. In 1888, he owned popular restaurant on East Gay, and was apparently doing well enough to place a full-age ad in the West Chester Board of Trade booklet. It read "Spence's Restaurant for Ladies and Gentlemen, the very Best Oysters Raw and Cooked, served in every Style."

One house important to African American history is a few doors up from the modest corner store once owned by a Jewish family. Danny Cohen ran a soda fountain and luncheonette there. The twin home at 143 East Miner could be described as Bayard Rustin's birthplace. It was where he lived as an infant with his teenage mother, Florence, and his grandparents, Janifer and Julia Rustin. They were living here when Rustin was born on March 17, 1912. According to Boyd's Directory, the entire family moved to 113 North New Street sometime between 1916 and 1917.

Facing page: *This former warehouse was recently restored. The mix of industrial and residential sites was typical here in the 19th century. Inset: James Spence's brother left the business by the time this ad ran.*

Above right: *A rare frame survivor on East Miner Street. Inset: Many of the buildings on East Miner still retain the Greek Revival-style small windows on the third floor.*

Ralston Hoopes Coal and Yard

200 block of South Matlack Street (now the Apartments for Modern Living)

Sometime in 1897, Hoopes replaced a rail siding here with a much larger one so that he had access to a side track from the main rail line. Afterwards, he advertised that his stove coal came "direct from the mines."

On the corner of Barnard and South Matlack, at what is now the Apartments for Modern Living, envision a very busy coal and lumber yard. In the 1850s, a man named John G. Robinson ran a coal and yard here with a partner named Shoemaker. Robinson also owned one of the row homes across the street, and he lived in a large house at 231-233 South Walnut where Ralston Hoopes later lived. It is interesting to note that Hoopes lived in Robinson's former home because Hoopes also acquired this coal/lumber site in 1874. A newspaper feature in 1914 described his extensive operation as the largest outside of Philadelphia.

Perhaps not surprisingly, considering Hoopes' reliance on the railroad, he wrote an editorial in 1897, urging local residents to allow the Pennsylvania Railroad company to establish a special train between Philadelphia and the borough, with no more than a few stops, so that local residents could consider commuting to work. The idea was to encourage West Chester's Board of Trade to establish more industries, drawing working men to borough. As Hoopes wrote, "it is a well-known fact that the laboring classes of any town are the inhabitants who make a place prosperous."

Above left: The main office of R.R. Hoopes is shown along Matlack looking towards Barnard is shown here. The two-wheeled horse carts were used to deliver stove coal.

Above right: During the years Ralston Hoopes owned his home, it had numerous decorative details including Palladian windows and a carved Eastlake-style cornice and dormers. The porch still retains its 221 wooden spindles.

Insets: R.R. Hoopes signed this receipt which advertised that the firm was located "below the Gas Works."

23

The Barnard Street Bridge Neighborhood

200 Block of South Matlack Street

GETTING THERE: The Barnard Street bridge and neighborhood is best reached by traveling down South Matlack from East Market and making a left on East Barnard.

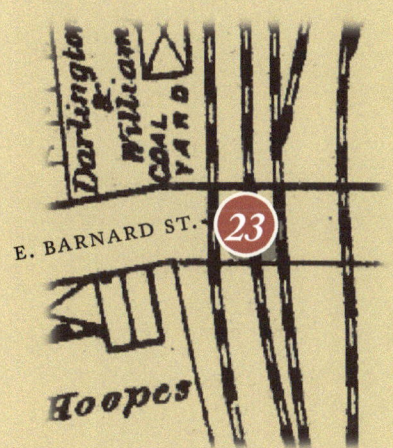

Another coal yard was located to the left of the Barnard Street Bridge. It backed into the West Chester Gas Works and in the 1880s was directly linked to the rail lines. The coal and lumber yards have been here for generations. From 1873 (Darlington & Williams) to the 1950s (J. Leon Hagerty). A man named Chalkey C. Hipple had it before Haggerty for several decades.

In his book *Railroads of West Chester,* Jim Jones describes the bridge was one of the first railroad bridges built in West Chester. Its construction in 1906 was prompted by numerous complaints about the dangerous crossing. It was especially tricky to navigate with a horse and wagon: one had to climb a steep grade here and then attempt to cross four sets of tracks.

By 1917 the bridge had to be widen to accommodate the numerous passenger and freight trains coming into the Market Street station. Additional tracks were needed to reduce congestion, as well as to serve the Hoopes Spokes Works, according to Jones.

In the 1940s, a small tavern known as "the Community Bar" stood at the northeast corner and at 113 East Barnard, Bayard Rustin's grandparents rented a house.

A reporter writing in September 11, 1946, noted that Rustin's grandparents granted him "permission" to have a meeting of the Committee of Racial Understanding here. On an 1883 map, the same lot is shown to be owned by Abram Dobson, the black journalist who was known for promoting a "life of equality" among former slaves.

Above right: Rustin's grandparents lived here in the mid-1940s They moved within a few years.

Additional tracks were added in 1917 to serve the Spokes Works.

Hoopes Spokes Works

Both sides of East Barnard extending to East Market (site now demolished)

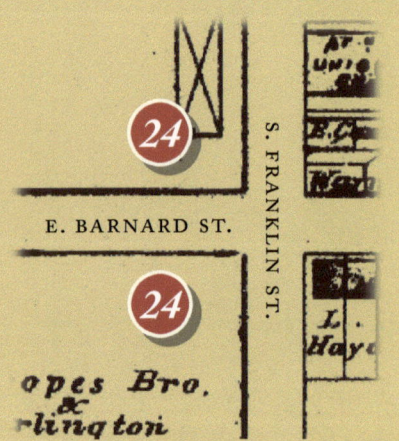

The company operated 24-hrs each day at its height in the late 1880s.

Imagine this entire area taken up by the massive brick structures of what was commonly called the "Hoopes Spokes Works." During its heyday in the 1800s, the firm was known internationally. Still, according to notices of the period, the firm never outgrew its modest origins. Metal rims were made at a forge along the French Creek, and mills in Birchrunville and Chester Springs supplied the company with logs that were milled on the premises. Even in 1880, when the company was operating 24 hours a day, one notice indicates, the workers took time out to supply a local club with archery bows.

In a 1992 interview, Betsy Hoopes Lawrence, whose late husband's family founded the firm, said that she still had the company's 1913 spring-wound time clock. Considering that in many ways the firm was a place where time stood still – it produced wheels until 1973 – a timepiece was an appropriate keepsake.

Top: The lumber shed and office were among a handful of frame buildings. Note the black workers in this c. 1870 photo. CCHS.

Inset at right: The rear of the Hoopes compex showing the boiler building. The early ads are courtesy of W. Supplee. Facing page: A collage by Amanda Craig.

The Locust Court Apartments

Corner of South Franklin, 200 and 300 Block of East Barnard

E. BARNARD ST.

This area was once dominated by single and twin brick homes.

In 1956, the *Daily Local News* reported the "shocking" results of a survey that was conducted under the newly formed Chester County Housing Committee. The survey covered living conditions in several communities in Chester County, including Downingtown, Coatesville, West Whiteland, and West Chester. The conclusion: The board found substandard housing is "a very serious problem for Chester County's Negro population."

It was the results of this survey that led to the establishment of Locust Court, the county's first public housing, although the actual groundbreaking ceremony did not take place until 1965. The complex included six buildings, with apartments units for the elderly and 36 row houses for families.

Above: The Locust Court Apartments as they looked in the 1960s. Photo by John Clark.

Inset: From a series of photographs including this one of an old house on Franklin, (labeled with the handwritten notes) were made in the 1920s by the League of Women Voters to determine the conditions of the neighborhood. Various views of the East End neighborhood, where backyards once featured hand-built sheds and vegetable gardens.

St. Luke U.A.M.E. Church
113 South Franklin Street

This church, which in its early years overlooked the Hoopes Spokes storage yards, was established in 1841. It was originally named Union A.M.E. and was located on East Union Street. At its present location, the church was intended to have 10 memorial windows (count the windows and see what you come up with!) On October 2, 1865, the church was dedicated and opened for divine services. Notice the beautiful glass window with a lotus leaf decoration below the date stone that was laid in 1865.

It was around that time that Moses G. Hepburn bought property here for $209.50 from the estate of George Washington, a veteran of the U.S. "Colored" Troops in the Civil War. It included a brick house facing Franklin on the corner of Barnard, with a stable behind it. He also acquired a brick building directly behind the church. It had access only by the alley so it must have used for storage for the nearby hotel. He was taxed for a 62-foot corner lot here in 1858 but it was described as a 120-foot lot in 1859. The tax records also described two dwellings "in the alley back of Franklin" on a 30-foot lot in 1875. A 1912 map shows this alley property to be owned by the church with the Hepburn dwellings gone.

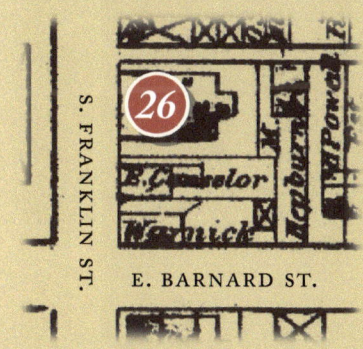
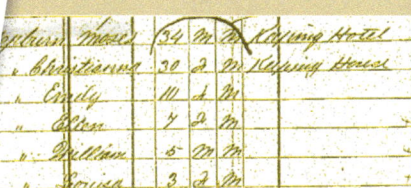

Above: Above: St. Luke's is known for its beautiful handcrafted memorial windows. They are similar in design to those at Bethel Church (site 4).
Inset: Members Emery Richardson and Vicky Ralph pose in front of St. Lukes.
Upper right: The borough tax of 1870 shows that Hepburn was taxed for "keeping a [public] house." His wife and four children are also listed.

The church was named for Luke Smith, an early leader of the congregation.

The Adams Street School

Northeast Corner of
East Barnard and Adams Streets
(site demolished)

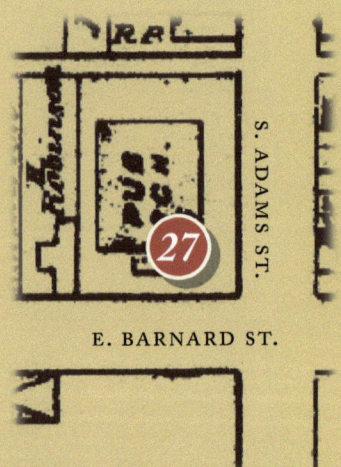

For many years, there were no black teachers at this all-black school.

West Chester's second public school – both of them for black children – was once located at the corner of Barnard and Adams. Many of these early schools were established after the Civil War specifically for black children. One black organization ahead of its time, the Harmony School Association, built its school in 1844.

The Harmony School, which had 54 black students in its first class, once stood opposite of Ben Freeman's house at 127 W. Barnard. When that school closed, students were sent to the Adams Street School, built around 1856. Interestingly, the school faced Barnard Street, but was named after the side street mainly to avoid confusion with the all-white public school, the Barnard Street School.

In a 1960 letter, Bayard Rustin recalled that his teachers at the Adams Street School were responsible for his longtime interest in history. "We all knew that [the town] was a stop on the Underground Railroad," he recalled, "We read Negro poetry and were steeped in the folk tales of our grandparents and great-grandparents.

When the Gay Street School opened in 1897, the Adams school housed various businesses including briefly as laundry owned by restauranteur Charles H. Burns. He was taxed for a dwelling on a 17 foot lot at #327 South Adams, and one horse in 1805.

Above: This circa 1889 photo of the Adams Street School by an early amateur photographer, J. Max Mueller. Photo courtesy of CCHS.

Inset: Henry Robinson, circa 1879. CCHS. He moved next door to the school after living in a "cabin" on South Franklin.

Star of West Tent

South Adams Street, between Barnard and Miner

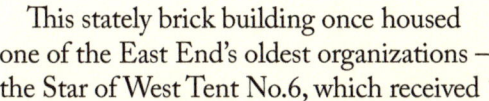

This stately brick building once housed one of the East End's oldest organizations – the Star of West Tent No.6, which received its charter in 1865. (Note: the building's date stone states that the group was established in 1864; it takes a year to get a charter.) Members built the building in 1879. It is designated with a historical marker, the only one in the East Ward, important not only because it mirrors the concerns of the early African American community, but because it reflects women's history in general. Tent No. 6 was founded at a time in the 1860s when women throughout the nation joined together and established literally thousands of organizations. It was part of a larger group called the United Order of Tents, now the oldest Christian fraternal organization organized entirely by women.

The organization was first founded by two Virginia slave women, "Sister" Annetta Lane and "Sister" Harriet R. Taylor, who selected the group's name and its symbol – a tent – to represent the "tent of salvation" for the African American community. Its early mission was described as "to clean, feed, and to provide nursing care wherever necessary" and members included former slaves known for their healing powers. In later years, members included registered and trained practical nurses who helped not only with the health of the community but raised funds for such necessaries as burial insurance for its members. This branch of order was established in 1847 in Philadelphia by an abolitionist congressman, J.R. Giddings and his law partner, Jollifee Union.

Above: The Star of West Tent is one of the few surviving buildings in the East End, offering a glimpse into what the community looked like in the years after the Civil War. It still stands next to an alley dating to the 1870s, when nearly every busy thoroughfare had an alley or service road.
Above left: The historical marker was dedicated in a special ceremony in 1995.
Above right: The building as it looks today. Inset: One of the symbols of the Star of West Tent.

GETTING THERE:
The Star of West Tent is closed to the public but can be best visited by taking S. Adams from East Market. The building will be on your left, before East Barnard.

The Star of West Tent is one of the few surviving post–Civil War buildings in the East End.

Around the Neighborhood

400 to 500 Block of East Barnard

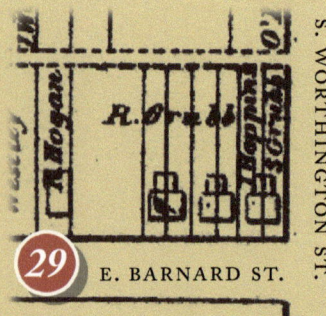

In the 1940s, the Nathan Holmes Post considered moving here.

A house that once stood at the northwest corner of Barnard and Adams was the original location of the "Day Nursery." It was organized in 1892 to accommodate the "colored" children whose mothers were housekeepers. This was a revolutionary concept – prior to the establishment of the nursery, the children were often left unattended. After this location, the nursery moved in 1886 to 137 East Market Street and again in 1889 to 126 East Market. When the nursery closed after being at this location for only a few years, the *Daily Local News* stated in that "no other institution of the town has been more helpful to the colored of this town." In its final years, the nursery charged families six cents a day for each child.

In 1846, the Nathan Holmes Post (#6 on the tour) considered moving here. They purchased land that had been the former play grounds of the Adams Street School but the plans fell through. At the time, the formerly all-black post was reorganized and membership "tripled." Two well-respected black educators were charter members: Joseph R. Fugett and Warren H. Burton, who was one of the founders of the legion's drum and bugle corps, organized in 1938.

Above right: Neighborhood children from the early twentieth century. Above left: Ephraim Spence, described as "colored" on the borough taxes, lived here in the late 1800s, with stabling behind the house. Inset: Advertisement for Spence's restaurant, once located uptown.

Burns' Great Oyster House and Dining Rooms.

Around the Neighborhood

600 to 700 Block of East Barnard

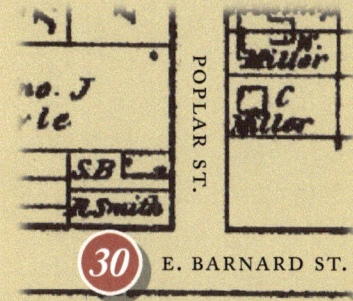

Not much is written about Rustin's mother and step-father, William Rustin, but they briefly lived together at 602 East Barnard in the 1930s. Another nearby Rustin home was 128 East Union. Rustin lived with his grandparents here during his senior year at West Chester High School.

It is not known if Charles H. Burns lived at 701 or 703, but he was taxed for these properties for several years beginning in 1905. The buildings do not appear on the 1915 tax or in 1917 when his estate listed only his "dwelling and store," the latter presumably his oyster bar on West Gay street (#4 on the "Uptown" map).

A notice in 1902 describes Burns' new laundry as located in the first floor of the school and powered by a 10-horse-power machine that ran a washer capable of cleaning 150 shirts, an "extractor, a "mangler," and a collar and cuff machine. Burns was best known, of course, for his "Great Oyster House" on West Gay, but he worked all his life in various enterprises including running a theater and making ice cream by the quart for take-out. His advertisements explained the concept, announcing "Nuff Sedd. Can you see the point?"

Another black entrepreneur James Spence is said to have lived above his restaurant in East Gay but he owned several houses in the East End. A relative, Ephraim Spence, listed on the early tax records as a "colored" laborer, lived at #427 East Barnard. In 1898, he was taxed for a dwelling, a frame stable and two horses.

Above left: Neighborhood homes once owned by Burns. Upper right: Burns, who looks white in this early newspaper illustration, stands in his kitchen.

The neighborhood included the grocery store, "Willy's."

31

Around the Neighborhood

Bolmar Street and
600 Block of East Miner

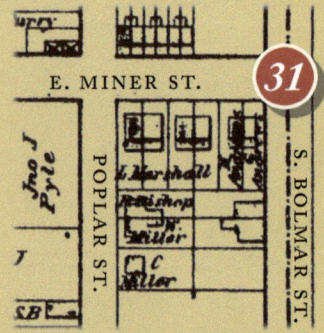

Bolmar Street is named for French school teacher, but the school closed before the East End was settled.

Bolmar Street has no historic structures today, but it's worth noting that the street was named for Antoine Brunin de Bolmar, a native of France, who ran a boy's school just north of East Biddle Street. Described by one paper as the "Napoleon of teachers," Bolmar took over the former Elmira H. Lincoln Phelps ladies seminary after the school failed in 1839. He taught his students, generally boarders from Philadelphia and the south, until the school closed in 1860.

As early as 1880, a notice headlined "Needs Looking After" described Bolmar Street between Market and Union as in major need of repair, urging the borough to act on the petition signed by local residents. In the mid-1800s, many of the houses were described in sheriff sales as "small" and "two-story frame" with "cellared, well of water, and a chain pump near the door."

In 1952, a series of newspaper stories described the "inadequate surface drainage" along Bolmar and East Union Streets, noting that the intersection was flooded with a three-foot deep, 200 foot long "lake." The "stagnant" lake developed after weeks of rain, the paper noted, "but nobody seems inclined to do much about it."

Above upper right and lower left: These houses are among the handful of Penn-style homes in the area. The "pink" house is unusual for its single windows in the front of the house and suggests it was once part of a twin.

Upper right: The community center circa 1962 as seen from Penn Street. The street appears on maps as early as 1873, although there were no houses.

32

Mt. Carmel Church of God in Christ

Corner of Bolmar and East Miner Street

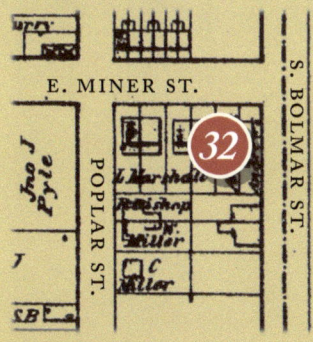

This church is one of the East End "newest" churches. It was established in 1963, when Jacob J. Meeks, along with his wife, Lenore and their three children, began a mission here. The entire congregation took part in the construction of this building.

Although the surrounding homes include new construction, many of the homes here date to the 1900s and are two-story brick dwellings. A notice in 1923 suggests that the several row houses facing Worthington and Poplar Streets were owned by one man – Harry F. Taylor – who rented a total of sixteen houses. Taylor bought the properties from the firm of Darlington & Marshall, making it the largest sale of dwelling houses in West Chester at the time. "These houses are 2-1/2 stories, of good size, of frame with yards attached," the paper reported.

In walking this section of the East End, notice that a few of the single homes are built on the Quaker or "Penn plan," with the front door to one side of two windows. These houses generally had three rooms on the first floor, with no foyer.

Around the corner on Poplar Street, there are several early homes. Ten of the homes on east side of the street were built in 1886 by John J. Pyle, called a "confectioner" in sales notices. He purchased the land as an investment sometime after 1883 and built ten 2-story framed houses. These new homes backed into the three twin homes Pyle built earlier on Worthington Street.

The entire congregation took part in the construction of this building.

33

Around the Neighborhood
South Worthington St.

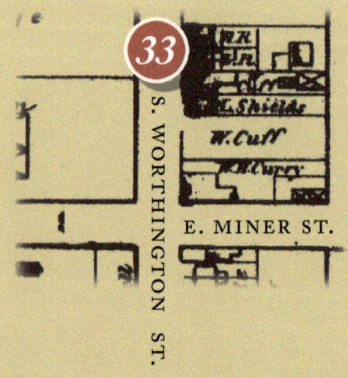

The 1883 map shows that William Cuff, a blacksmith, had a lot, dwelling and stables along South Worthington.

On the 1873 Witmer's Atlas, only a handful of houses are found along South Worthington Street. By 1884, a row of houses stood where the present-day Milestones is located.

A notice in 1906, announced that Solomon Hazard, who is described as a blacksmith on the tax records, was adding a new porch to his house and "making other repairs." He may have retired by the time he was living here. The 1883 map shows that William Cuff, a blacksmith, had a lot, dwelling and stables along South Worthington.

Cuff lived in a brick dwelling facing Worthington and also owned a lot (perhaps used as pastureland) a door down from L.W. Shields, who owned a plaster and gravel supply business and employed Benjamin Freeman as a hauler.

Other names scattered throughout the tax lists for the East End include George W. Smith, a former bartender of Magnolia House; John Draper, barber; Ben Thomas, grocer; Cato Smith, laborer; John Bond, huckster; and Joshua Pierce, who once described himself as the "only colored Pierce" in West Chester.

Above left: In the 1800s, the homes seen beyond the playing fields include the home of Levi Hood and William Cuff, a blacksmith.

Lower right: On the 1873 Witmer's Atlas, only a handful of houses are found on South Worthington street. The lots today are part of the DeBaptist complex. In more recent times, a post office stood at the corner of East Market and Worthington Streets.

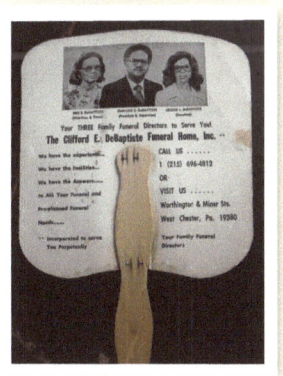

DeBaptiste Funeral Home

601 East Miner Street

This long-time family operation had its start in 1954 at 124 East Barnard Street and has always lived up to its motto: "Up-to-date facilities, Old Fashioned Dignity and Everyday Economy."

The funeral home was founded by Clifford DeBaptiste and Inez E. Manning DeBaptiste. As the business grew, they relocated to the corner of Worthington & Miner Streets and later opened a second funeral home in Bryn Mawr.

This site was built by renowned African-American contractor Mr. Lawrence Derry, and opened its doors to the public during the "Great January blizzard" of 1965. Mrs. DeBaptiste and her daughter, Lillian, successfully completed all the requirements to become funeral directors.

In 1993, Clifford E. DeBaptiste was the first African American to be elected mayor of West Chester. He was re-elected in 1997. DeBaptist expanded his business in recent years to include the "Milestone Events" complex.

Above: Notice the unusually tall and narrow house at the corner of the DeBaptiste complex. This house, built sometime in the late 1880s, was once the home of William H. Curry, who was a grocer and oyster seller.

GETTING THERE:
The DeBaptist complex is best reached from East Market Street, taking either Poplar Street or South Bolmar and then right on East Miner. Parking is on your right.

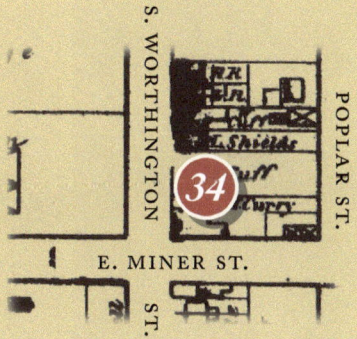

Early homes here once included that of Levi M. Hood.

Important Sites Outside the East End

The former Gay Street School

401 East Gay Street

(site demolished)
The site is now occupied by West Chester's borough hall

For generations, the Gay Street School has been a source of pride – and sometimes pain. The school brought people together, former students say, and, at the same time, kept them apart. The school, simply named for its location, Gay Street, was West Chester's only public elementary school for African American children. It was Pennsylvania's oldest segregated school. And in 1957, it was the last in the state to be integrated.

"Our parents were dedicated to education, but it wasn't their decision to send their children to the Gay Street School," Dot Jackson said in a 1997 interview for the *Philadelphia Inquirer*. "You went there regardless of where you lived in the borough."

The school's most famous alumnus was Bayard Rustin. However, there were a number of graduates who became either a community activist or the only "first" in the community. In years past, the annual alumni dinner celebration has honored John O. Green, who became West Chester's first black chief of police in the mid-1970s, Mildred R. Barkley, who, in 1953, became the first African American to be hired on the nursing staff at Chester County Hospital, Ray Vernon Spriggs, the first African-American in the Peace Corps, Dr. Cornelius H. Gaither, the borough's first black dentist, and Dr. W.T.M. Johnson, a community activist who in 1984 successfully challenged an at-large election system whose effect was that no African Americans had been elected to borough office for more than 90 years.

Most residents of the East End today remember Joseph Fugett, a beloved principal who assembled an inspiring faculty during his years at the school from 1920 to 1955. The teachers included Maria Brock and Helena Robinson.

Even before the school opened in 1897, controversy blazed a trail of discussion in local newspapers. Many black residents were concerned that there were plenty of qualified black teachers, but those who were hired were white and were from outside the community. One account in 1894, reported that all the "colored people" were dissatisfied that "West Chester is the only town in the state where the color line is so tightly drawn in the public school."

Following protests and petitions by parents and other community people who insisted on black children being taught by leaders of their own race, the Gay Street School opened and replaced the Adams Street School. Three teachers at Gay Street were hired, but none of them studied at a teaching college. All three graduated from West Chester High School at the other part of town, where Bayard Rustin attended high school.

In 1908, the Gay Street School was partly destroyed by fire. The school made headlines again when the borough considered building a new school on the site of the old Adams Street School. James Spence, a black restaurateur, published a poem for the occasion, the first lines of which read: "Give us back our Gay Street School house. Build it up; it is our pride." The building was demolished to build the present borough structure in the early 1990s. Much of its original stone was reportedly recycled and used to build the present-day apartments along Patton Alley.

Top Left Page Left to Right:

Warren H. Burton, the tall man in the far right in the last row, was coach of the football team at the time of this picture. He is often cited as a major influence on Bayard Rustin. Courtesy of CCHS.

The Gay Street Public School was built in 1895 after the Adams Street School closed. Its unusual, fortress-like design was the brainchild of architect (and West Chester native) Arthur Ebbs Willauer. Postcard courtesy of William Supplee.

The Gay Street School as depicted on an early postcard. Joseph R. Fugett was perhaps the best known principal, serving from 1920-1955. Postcard courtesy of William Supplee.

The Gay Street School was partly destroyed by a fire in 1908 but otherwise retained its massive size. It was demolished to make way for the present-day Borough Hall in the 1990s.

The various class pictures of the Gay Street school date from the 1900s, 1920s, and 1930s.

Important Sites Outside the East End

Horace Pippin's Home
327 West Gay Street

A historic marker was placed here on June 9, 1979, recognizing Pippin's creativity during the years he lived in the house, from the 1920s until his death in 1946, at the age of 58.

As early as 1941, critics cited both Pippin's wooden-panel paintings and his canvas works, typically created with ordinary house paint and bedticking, as an example of the "make-do" attitude of a self-taught artist who once explained that he saw "pictures" in his head.

Before he was "discovered" by the art collector, Albert C. Barnes, in late 1930s, Pippin sold many of his local scenes, informally, much like a fruit vendor, by propping them against a chair in front of his home. Less than a decade later, a "choice Pippin," as one paper in 1944 reported, could command a price of more than $1,000. Still, the same work that is regarded today as a window into the heritage of African Americans was hailed in Pippin's day merely as sign of unencumbered self-expression.

Interestingly, Pippin's first "official" art display was in the borough at the Chester County Art Association on June 8, 1937. The two-week group show featured the young Andrew Wyeth, but it attracted a record 2,550 people in part because of Pippin. Indeed, two days after the show closed, Barnes and Wyeth's father, N. C. Wyeth, arranged for Pippin to exhibit in a solo show at the West Chester Community Center.

The opening reception included talks by the art critic Christian Brinton, and Dr. Leslie Pinckney Hill, president of Cheyney State Teachers College. Bayard Rustin, Pippin's former neighbor who was then a student at Cheyney, was the featured tenor soloist.

Above: Pippin completed the majority of his art work here during his years of residency, from the 1920s until his death in 1946.

Upper left inset: This beautiful house, once occupied by the Jackson family, stands opposite of the Pippin home on West Gay Street. From the 1950s and through the early part of 1960s, Dot Jackson hosted many activities for women including garden parties.

Lower inset: The backyard of the former Rustin home, at 315 West Gay, can be seen to the right of this small child (co-author Sarah Wesley).

West Chester High School

North Church Street and West Washington Streets (site demolished)

This circa 1906 postcard depicts the newly open West Chester High School. Just out of view, at left, is the Biddle Street School (an elementary school). It was known as the "old Church Street School" when it was built in 1863. The original Biddle Street School is now an apartment complex. Postcard courtesy of William Supplee.

For generations, West Chester High was the only non-segregated school in the borough. Curiously, it featured separate entrances for "boys" and "girls." When Bayard Rustin attended the school, from 1928 to 1932, the front entrance was dubbed the "senior steps" and open only to seniors.

The original high school, which had its first graduating class in 1866, was razed in 1917, and built anew as the "Biddle Street School" (made from recycled bricks). A new high school was built next door. It was considered the most modern school of its day, complete with science labs, the region's first school library, classrooms devoted to sewing and drawing, and a commercial department with typewriters.

West Chester High was integrated from the start but black students were often unprepared to study in its advanced classes, in part because of a requirement that they complete 7th and 8th grade at the Gay Street School and then transfer to Biddle Street for their final year of junior high. Students typically found themselves lacking in required subjects such as algebra, which wasn't taught at the Gay Street School.

Rustin faced the same problem with the added disadvantage: the state-of-the-art "Auditorium School," where he might have sang, was not built until years after he graduated. Sadly, the building was razed as part of the school district's consolidation plan after the high school was destroyed by fire in 1947.

Above, right: The former "Auditorium School," built in 1937 by the Works Progress Administration (WPA). It housed a cafeteria, 7th grade classrooms and an enormous stage with an orchestra pit.

Inset Left: The Biddle School and West Chester High, in the foreground, once stood side-by-side on Church Street.

Inset Right: The "Senior Steps" at the high school.

About the Authors

Catherine Quillman and Sarah Wesley

Catherine Quillman is a former suburban staff writer for *The Philadelphia Inquirer*, where she covered the arts and wrote numerous history pieces on the little known aspects of West Chester and Chester County, Pennsylvania. She has lived in the borough since 1994, and is now a freelance arts reporter and magazine writer.

She is the author of five regional books including the recently published art book, *100 Artists of the Brandywine Valley*. She also helps other writers with the print-on-demand publishing process. To learn more, visit www.quillman-publications.

Sarah Wesley is a native of West Chester whose writing and artistic career has included working at the Chester County Historical Society (CCHS) and serving as the main coordinator for an annual African-American Art Show that benefited a local NAACP scholarship fund.

Her community work has focused on helping young people connect with local black history. This has included writing and editing "*Word*," an African-American history newsletter for which she was honored by the black student union at Henderson High School in West Chester.

Sarah was instrumental in drawing attention to the historical importance of the Star of West Tent to obtain a State Historical Marker there – the only marker of its kind in the East End. She also assisted in the scholarship and community outreach for two award-winning exhibits at CCHS, "Between Women," and "Just Over the Line: Chester County and the Underground Railroad." Her work with CCHS (where she was employed for 15 years) also led her to write the original walking tour that formed the basis of this book.